AMAZING AMERICA

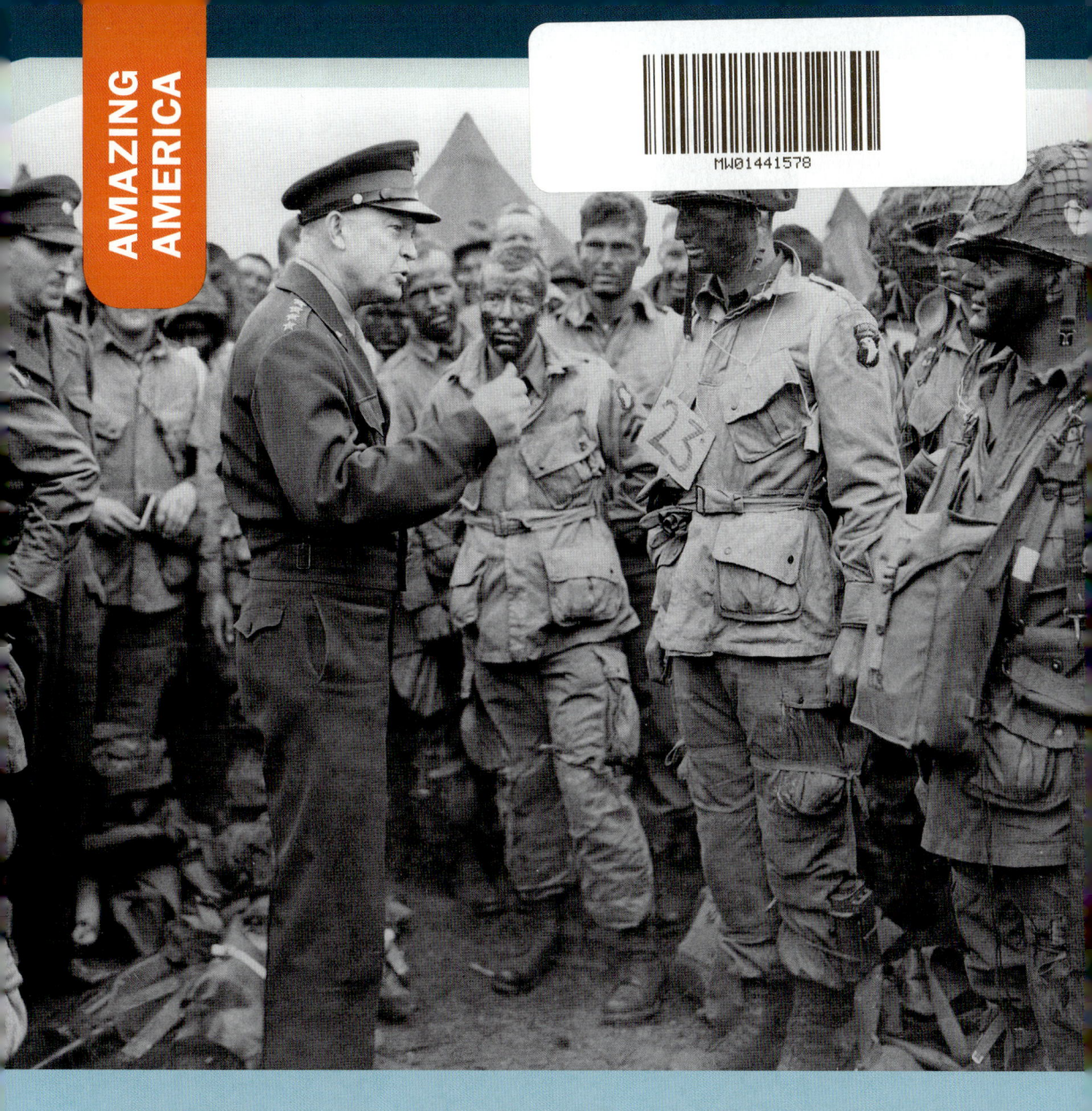

THE 12 MOST AMAZING
AMERICAN BATTLES

by Anita Yasuda

12 STORY LIBRARY

www.12StoryLibrary.com

Copyright © 2015 by Peterson Publishing Company, North Mankato, MN 56003. All rights reserved. No part of this book may be reproduced or utilized in any form or by any means without written permission from the publisher.

12-Story Library is an imprint of Peterson Publishing Company and Press Room Editions.

Produced for 12-Story Library by Red Line Editorial

Photographs ©: Library of Congress, cover, 1, 8, 10, 14, 24; Detroit Publishing Company/Library of Congress, 4; Cornelius Tiebout/Library of Congress, 5; John Norman/Library of Congress, 6; Percy Moran/Library of Congress, 7, 12; N. Currier/Library of Congress, 9; Illman Brothers/Library of Congress, 11; Carol Highsmith/Library of Congress, 13; Currier & Ives/Library of Congress, 15; Henry Alexander Ogden/Library of Congress, 16; Paul Philippoteaux/Library of Congress, 17; Frederic Remington/Library of Congress, 18; Zack Frank/Shutterstock Images, 19; US Navy/Library of Congress, 20, 29; AP Images, 21; Bettmann/Corbis, 22, 23; US Maritime Commission/AP Images, 25; Bob Campbell/Defense Department/AP Images, 26; Joe Rosenthal/AP Images, 27

ISBN
978-1-63235-006-0 (hardcover)
978-1-63235-066-4 (paperback)
978-1-62143-047-6 (hosted ebook)

Library of Congress Control Number: 2014937238

Printed in the United States of America
Mankato, MN
June, 2017

Go beyond the book. Get free, up-to-date content on this topic at 12StoryLibrary.com.

TABLE OF CONTENTS

Battles of Lexington and Concord 4

Battle of Bunker Hill 6

Battles of Saratoga 8

Siege of Yorktown 10

Battle of the Alamo 12

Battle of Antietam 14

Battle of Gettysburg 16

Battle of Little Bighorn 18

Attack on Pearl Harbor 20

Battle of Midway 22

Invasion of Normandy 24

Battle of Iwo Jima 26

Fact Sheet 28

Glossary 30

For More Information 31

Index 32

About the Author 32

1

AMERICAN REVOLUTION STARTS WITH BATTLES OF LEXINGTON AND CONCORD

By 1775, many American colonists had decided they wanted independence from Great Britain. They started to gather militiamen and weapons for a possible war. Great Britain sent General Thomas Gage to put down the rebellion. Gage and 700 British soldiers set off for Concord, Massachusetts. Their plan was to destroy the colonists' weapon stash there.

On April 19, 1775, the redcoats arrived in Lexington. They were surprised to find 70 militiamen waiting for them. The two sides faced off across the town square. The British yelled at the colonial militiamen to lay down their arms. Then a shot was fired. Both sides began firing. Moments later, eight militiamen were dead. Nine were wounded.

The British marched on to Concord. There they searched for guns and supplies. But the colonists had been warned. They had already moved most of their supplies before the British arrived. In the meantime,

The Minute Man statue in Concord was created for the one-hundredth anniversary of the battle.

hundreds of militiamen gathered. They rushed the British. The fighting was over quickly. Two colonial soldiers and three British soldiers died. The British retreated to Boston. Colonial militiamen attacked them from all sides as they marched back. The militiamen hid behind trees, rocks, and homes. By the time the British made it back to Boston, 273 British soldiers had been killed or wounded.

Colonial militiamen fire on the British in Lexington.

4
Hours the British soldiers searched for weapons and supplies in Concord before fighting broke out.

- April 19, 1775
- First fighting of the American Revolution.
- 275 British casualties and 95 colonial casualties.
- The colonial militiamen forced the British to retreat.
- Within months, thousands of colonists joined the Continental Army.

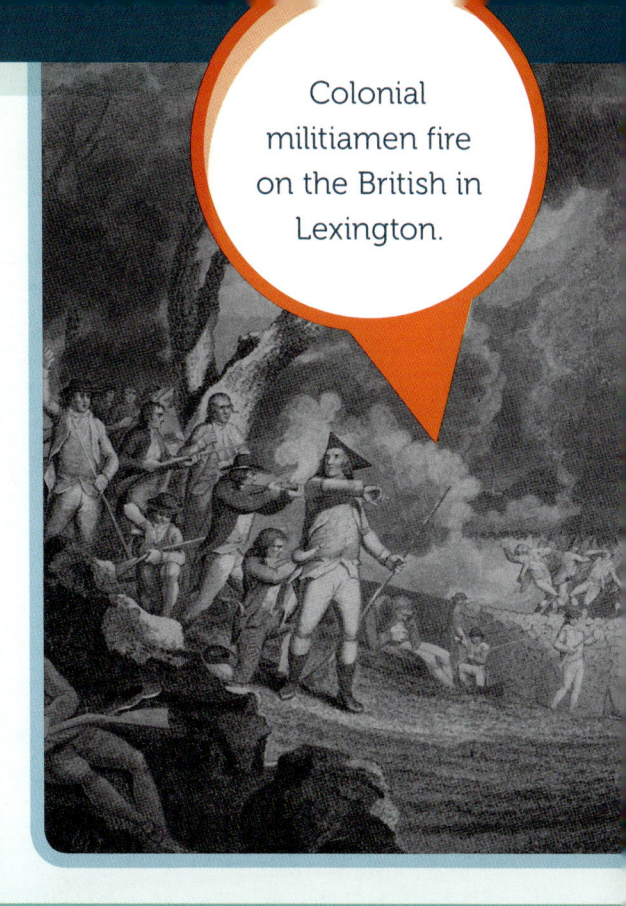

REVERE'S RIDE

Paul Revere was a silversmith who supported the American colonists' fight for independence. Revere, William Dawes, and Samuel Prescott carried messages for the American colonists. On April 18, Revere and Dawes rode separately to Lexington to warn the patriots that the British were coming. After they were stopped by British patrols, Prescott carried the message to Concord.

BRITISH WIN COSTLY BATTLE OF BUNKER HILL

As the American Revolution started, the British planned to take control of Bunker and Breed's Hills. The hills were just across the water from Boston. The colonists heard of the plan. They decided to seize control of Bunker Hill before the British had a chance. Traveling in the dark, the colonial troops mistakenly ended up on Breed's Hill instead.

Colonel William Prescott and his men worked all night. They dug trenches and built dirt walls. They put up fences and dug pits. They hoped these obstacles would slow down the more experienced British forces. On June 17, 1775, General Thomas Gage sent British troops to take the hill. The redcoats rushed the hill with their bayonets. But the colonial soldiers hid in trenches and behind walls. They shot British soldiers as they were coming up the hill.

Colonial general Joseph Warren died in the Battle of Bunker Hill.

THINK ABOUT IT

The colonial troops meant to fortify Bunker Hill but ended up on Breed's Hill by mistake. How do you think the troops got lost? What kind of tools do you think troops in the 1700s may have been using to find their way?

The Battle of Bunker Hill actually took place on Breed's Hill.

More British soldiers charged the hill. The colonists ran out of ammunition. They fought with clubs, fists, and rocks. Finally, the British forced them to flee. Although the colonists lost, the damage they did to the British forces gave them confidence to keep fighting the war.

3

Number of times the British troops stormed Breed's Hill during the battle.

- June 17, 1775
- Approximately 1,200 colonial soldiers defended their position against 2,100 British troops.
- The colonists had 411 casualties.
- The British had more than 1,000 casualties.

PETER SALEM

Peter Salem was an African-American soldier. He was born a slave. After he was freed, he became a minuteman for the American colonists. Salem fought at Breed's Hill. His last shot killed British major John Pitcairn. His actions allowed others to flee. Salem stayed with the army until the end of the war.

BATTLES OF SARATOGA TURN TIDE OF REVOLUTION

In the third year of the American Revolution, British general John Burgoyne pushed his army toward Albany, New York. The British wanted to cut off New England from the other rebelling American colonies. But colonial troops under the command of General Horatio Gates stood in Burgoyne's way.

On September 19, 1777, the sound of drums signaled the British attack. The colonial troops were ready. The armies met at Freeman's Farm near Saratoga, New York. Soon, thick smoke covered the fields. The fighting lasted all day. As night arrived, the colonists fell back.

On October 7, Burgoyne attacked again. Gates had set up cannons on the highest hill, Bemis Heights. After another day of fighting, British casualties were high, and

General Horatio Gates is best known for his success at Saratoga.

8,000

British troops who marched toward Albany, New York.

- September 19 and October 7, 1777
- The colonial army grew from 12,000 to 20,000 as reinforcements arrived.
- Fighting took place in New York state at Freeman's Farm, Bemis Heights, and Saratoga.
- Colonial victory is considered a major turning point in the war.

HESSIANS

The British needed soldiers to fight in America. They paid German soldiers to fight for them. These men were called Hessians. Approximately 30,000 Hessians fought in the American Revolution. Some made the United States their home after the war.

supplies were running low. The 5,000 remaining British troops retreated to Saratoga. Approximately 20,000 colonial troops surrounded the British forces there. Greatly outnumbered, Burgoyne surrendered to General Gates on October 17. The British army continued to fight in the South. But this was a major victory for the colonies in the North. Afterward, France decided to enter the war on the colonies' side.

British general John Burgoyne surrenders at Saratoga.

4

SIEGE OF YORKTOWN ENDS AMERICAN REVOLUTION

After six years of fighting in the American Revolution, British general Charles Cornwallis was leading his troops to Yorktown, Virginia. From there, he thought they could raid nearby towns. He could also wait there for British supply ships. However, General George Washington decided to block him. He marched his men to Yorktown. French troops joined them.

The two armies trapped the British. They worked all night to dig a trench

> German Hessian soldiers fought on the side of the British at Yorktown.

close to the British line. It was more than one mile (1.6 km) long. Troops poured into the trenches. They brought cannons with them.

Cornwallis saw that the British were outnumbered. They tried to escape across the river to New Jersey. A bad storm made them turn their boats back. Then French ships arrived. The French trapped the British navy. Cornwallis's men would not be able to escape by sea. The British army had no way out. The American and French troops hammered the British troops with cannon fire. Cornwallis surrendered on October 19, 1781.

8,000
British troops who were taken prisoner by the end of the siege.

- September 18–October 19, 1781
- Approximately 14,000 French and colonial troops combined to overpower the British.
- The British surrender at Yorktown ended fighting in the American Revolution.

British general Charles Cornwallis surrenders at Yorktown.

5

TEXANS FIGHT FOR INDEPENDENCE AT THE ALAMO

In 1836, Texas was a territory of the country of Mexico. Texans were determined to fight to become their own independent nation. Approximately 200 Texans occupied the Alamo, a former mission and military fort in San Antonio. A small number of women and children accompanied them. Several thousand Mexican soldiers arrived on February 23, 1836, and laid siege to the Alamo. The Mexicans wanted to take back control of San Antonio.

For 12 days, the small Texan forces held off the Mexican army. The Mexicans shot cannons at the Alamo's walls. The Texans fired back with muskets, rifles, and cannons. They forced the Mexican army back. But the Texans were too badly outnumbered. And reinforcements never came.

On March 6, 1836, the Mexican soldiers silently moved into position. General Antonio López de Santa Anna gave them the signal to strike.

A painting shows Texans defending the Alamo.

The Alamo is now a museum.

He raised a red flag, which meant that the soldiers should not take any prisoners. The Mexican army rushed the walls. Soon, the sounds of gunfire and yelling filled the air. Women and children hid from the fight. The Texans fought with rifles, knives, and even their bare hands. They refused to surrender. But the Mexican army overran them. Almost all the Texans were killed within two hours. Approximately 15 Texans, mostly women and children, survived. "Remember the Alamo" became a battle cry for Texans who wanted independence from Mexico. They won it six weeks later at the Battle of San Jacinto.

12
Days the Alamo was under siege.

- February 23–March 6, 1836
- Approximately 200 Texans occupied the Alamo.
- The number of Mexican troops has been estimated between 1,800 and 6,000.
- Between 600 and 1,600 Mexicans were killed in the battle. Almost all the Texans died.

DEFENDING THE ALAMO

The Texans pushed dirt against the Alamo's walls. They hoped the thicker walls would stop the cannonballs. They rolled cannons up these dirt ramps. One was fired three times a day in case reinforcements were near. The cannon blasts showed that the fort had not yet been taken.

6

UNION WINS BLOODY VICTORY IN BATTLE OF ANTIETAM

A year into the Civil War, Union general Joseph Hooker stood by Miller's Farm, near Sharpsburg, Maryland. As Hooker looked out, a glimmer in the cornfields caught his eye. It was sunlight shining on bayonets. At once, he knew the field was filled with Confederate soldiers. The Confederate army was trying to advance toward Washington, DC. Hooker ordered his army to open fire. The fighting was frantic. Waves of troops tried to control the field near Antietam Creek. Bullets whistled and hissed over

Union troops take control of the bridge over Antietam Creek.

EMANCIPATION PROCLAMATION

Lincoln decided to issue the Emancipation Proclamation in the summer of 1862. But he was waiting until a big victory put the Union in a strong position. On September 22, he told the Confederates to surrender by the end of the year. If they did not, he would free all slaves living in Confederate states. Lincoln officially issued the proclamation on January 1, 1863. Because Confederate states were not under Union control, very few slaves were freed at that time.

General George McClellan led the Union army in the Battle of Antietam.

soldiers' heads. Cannonballs sailed through the air. The ground shook.

The fighting went on for many hours. Late in the day, Confederate soldiers hid in a country road that had sunk below ground level. As Union soldiers advanced, the Confederates easily shot them down at first. But the Union troops continued until they had the Confederate soldiers surrounded. Almost 2,000 Confederate soldiers were trapped and killed on what became known as Bloody Lane. The day ended with 13,724 Confederate casualties and 12,410 Union casualties. It was the single bloodiest day in US history.

The next day, Confederate general Robert E. Lee retreated with the rest of his troops to Virginia. They had lost their best chance to attack the US capital. A few days after the Union victory at Antietam, President Abraham Lincoln announced the Emancipation Proclamation.

26,134
Troops on both sides who were killed, wounded, or listed as missing.

- September 17, 1862
- Fought near Antietam Creek, a branch of the Potomac River.
- Approximately 60,000 soldiers fought for the Union.
- Approximately 30,000 soldiers fought for the Confederacy.

7

BATTLE OF GETTYSBURG STOPS CONFEDERATE INVASION

After two years of fighting the Civil War, Confederate general Robert E. Lee decided to invade the North. The Confederates hoped to discourage the North from continuing to fight the Civil War. They also wanted European countries to recognize the Confederacy. Lee entered southwestern Pennsylvania with an army of 75,000. They met the Union army at Gettysburg on July 1, 1863. Cannons fired and artillery poured down. It sounded like a thunderstorm. Thick smoke darkened the sky. For two days, the two armies battled for positions. Wave after wave of attacks resulted in high casualties on both sides.

By the morning of July 3, 1863, only a mile of open fields separated the two sides. The Union command hoped to trick the Confederates into coming out into the open. They stopped firing their cannons. Their plan worked.

General Lee believed the Union's cannons had been wiped out. He ordered a division to charge the center of the line. It was led by

Confederate general George Pickett receives his orders to lead a charge.

16

THINK ABOUT IT

President Abraham Lincoln delivered the Gettysburg Address four months after the Battle of Gettysburg. What message did he deliver and how did it relate to the battle?

George Pickett. Pickett's 13,000 men rushed across the open field. Bullets zipped through the wheat. And Union cannons began firing again. More than half of Pickett's troops died. Lee's plan had failed. His soldiers were worn out. They returned to Virginia, ending their invasion of the North.

23,000

Approximate Union casualties over three days. The Confederates had approximately 28,000 casualties.

- July 1–3, 1863
- General George Meade led 88,000 Union troops.
- General Robert E. Lee led 75,000 Confederate troops.
- The battle ended the Confederates' invasion of the North.

More than 160,000 troops fought in the Battle of Gettysburg.

8

CUSTER DEFEATED AT BATTLE OF LITTLE BIGHORN

In 1868, a treaty granted land west of the Missouri River to Plains Indians, including the Dakota and Cheyenne peoples. But white miners searching for gold wanted to settle there. The US government ordered the Dakota Indians to move to reservations by 1876. When they did not, the government sent troops.

Colonel George Custer's cavalry searched for encampments on the Little Bighorn River. On the morning of June 25, 1876, Custer's scouts found a Dakota/Cheyenne village. Approximately 6,000 people lived in the village. Custer thought they might scatter if he waited for backup.

Custer divided his cavalry, planning to attack from all sides. Major Marcus Reno's troops reached the

George Custer, *kneeling on left*, and several of his soldiers fire at the Plains Indians during the Battle of Little Bighorn.

18

camp first. Surprised, the Cheyenne and Dakota warriors ran for their arms. They leapt onto horses and shot back at the soldiers, driving them back. Reno retreated, joining with troops led by Captain Frederick Benteen. In the meantime, Custer approached with the rest of the troops toward the far side of camp. As Reno retreated, the warriors focused on Custer's men. The US troops were greatly outnumbered. All of Custer's men were killed within an hour. Afterward, the US government flooded the area with troops. The Dakota and Cheyenne peoples were forced to surrender.

The site where Custer and his men were buried has been designated a national cemetery.

209
Men led into battle by Custer, all of whom were killed. Of the 400 troops led by other commanders, 53 were killed and 60 wounded.

- June 25–26, 1876
- US troops faced approximately 1,000 to 1,500 Cheyenne and Dakota warriors.
- Approximately 30 Dakota and Cheyenne warriors were killed in battle. So were six women and four children.
- Also called Custer's Last Stand.

VISION OF VICTORY

A few weeks before the battle, Chief Sitting Bull held a Native American ceremony called the Sun Dance. Sitting Bull danced, sang, and prayed. He cut his flesh and did not drink anything for two days. Afterward, he said he had a vision of soldiers falling into the camp upside down. The Dakota thought this vision meant they were going to win a big battle soon.

9

JAPAN LAUNCHES SURPRISE ATTACK ON PEARL HARBOR

On December 7, 1941, Japanese planes swooped down from the skies. A few people in Pearl Harbor, Hawaii, heard them roaring overhead. Some looked up and saw a red sun painted on the planes' wings. It represented the Japanese flag. At first, people thought it was a drill. It wasn't. The planes began dropping bombs on US aircraft and ships. More waves of Japanese planes came. They took out buildings and hospital tents.

The Pearl Harbor naval base and the USS *Shaw* were ablaze after the Japanese attack.

8

US battleships damaged in the raid. All but two were repaired and returned to service.

- December 7, 1941
- Attack started at 7:55 a.m.
- 3,400 US casualties, with more than 2,400 killed.
- Fewer than 100 Japanese casualties.

THINK ABOUT IT

President Franklin Roosevelt called the Pearl Harbor attack "a day which will live in infamy." What do you think he meant? What are some other dates in history that could be described this way?

Soon, huge fireballs lit up the morning sky. Clouds of smoke rose. US Navy ships opened fire. Several US fighter jets took off. They shot down dozens of Japanese planes. When the attack was over, half the American fleet of ships and hundreds of planes were destroyed. More than 2,000 people were killed.

The next day, the United States declared war on Japan. Three days later, Japanese allies Germany and Italy declared war on the United States.

Smoke rises from the battleship USS *Arizona* as it sinks.

10

BATTLE OF MIDWAY IS TURNING POINT IN WORLD WAR II

Four Japanese ships sailed towards Midway Island during World War II. The island housed a small American base. The Japanese wanted to destroy the US naval fleet in the Pacific and take the base. From there, they could more easily strike Hawaii again. But the Americans had figured out the code the Japanese used to discuss their plans. Three US aircraft carriers were waiting for them at Midway Island.

On June 4, 1942, approximately 90 Japanese planes attacked. The US Navy was ready. They returned fire from the ground. American planes quickly took off. But the Japanese planes were newer and faster than the US aircraft. It was easy for them to shoot down the older American planes.

At the same time, the Japanese aircraft carriers had been spotted. Planes from the US carriers began

An American aircraft carrier goes up in flames after Japanese planes attacked.

22

their attack. The first wave of US bombers was destroyed. But then the Japanese planes returned to the aircraft carriers for refueling. The next wave of US bombers surprised the Japanese. Within minutes, three Japanese carriers went up in flames. Americans sent the fourth carrier to the bottom of the sea the next day. More than 3,000 Japanese troops died. As a result of the losses, Japan ended its invasion of the Pacific. The US Navy continued capturing islands, moving closer to Japan.

US Navy planes attack during the height of the battle.

150

US planes that were destroyed. More than 300 Japanese aircraft were destroyed.

- June 3–6, 1942
- Battle took place mostly in the air.
- Japan lost most of its aircraft carriers and its best pilots.
- One US aircraft carrier was destroyed. Japan lost four carriers.

CODE BREAKER

Joe Rochefort worked for US intelligence. He broke the Japanese naval code and gave the US military daily updates on Japan's plans. Rochefort figured out that the Japanese military called Midway "AF." Then he heard them talking about plans to attack AF. Rochefort warned the US Navy so they could be ready.

23

11

ALLIES FREE FRANCE WITH INVASION OF NORMANDY

In June 1944, US troops were preparing to take the beaches of Normandy, France. Canadian and British troops, allied with the Americans, were stationed to the north. The Allied forces wanted to liberate France from the Germans. Then they could attack Germany. Ahead of them lay a heavily armed 50-mile (80-km) stretch of beach.

GHOST ARMY

The Allies wanted to trick the Germans into thinking they were attacking in places they were not. A group known as the Ghost Army set up fake army camps. The camps had dummy tanks, jeeps, and aircraft. They used sound effects to make them seem real. Planes dropped dolls with parachutes. Each exploded when it neared the ground. Before the invasion of Normandy, Germans thought the Allied forces were attacking on a different beach.

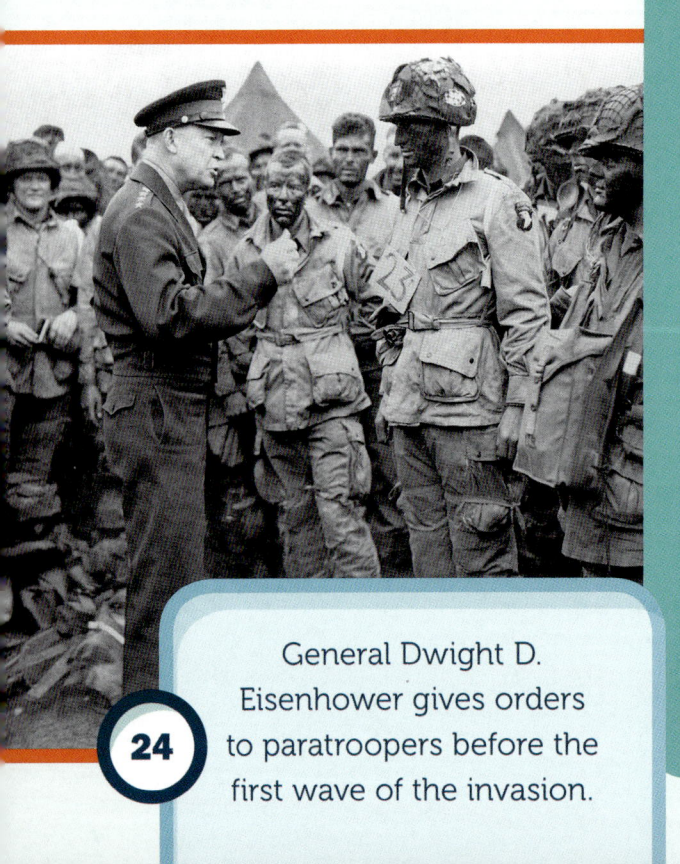

General Dwight D. Eisenhower gives orders to paratroopers before the first wave of the invasion.

Landing craft carrying Allied troops approach the beaches of Normandy.

Airborne troops dropped behind enemy lines. Many were killed, but others kept fighting. They destroyed some of the Germans' weaponry and captured key roads and bridges. Then thousands of planes dropped bombs on German targets.

Back at the beaches, thousands of Allied troops jumped from landing craft into the water. The waters were full of mines. Vehicles called minesweepers cleared a path to the beach. Under heavy fire, the Allied troops ran for the beach. The fighting at Omaha Beach was brutal. American troops faced steep cliffs and bluffs. A German infantry division hammered them. Slowly, the Americans moved forward. They took out the German guns. Together with the Allies, they broke through the German defenses. By the end of August 1944, Allied troops had freed France and were moving into Nazi Germany.

2,000
Americans killed on the first day of battle.

- Launched on June 6, 1944
- Approximately 160,000 Allied troops stormed five beaches in Normandy, France.
- The military operation was called Operation Overlord. It was also known as D-Day.

US CAPTURES MILITARY BASE AT IWO JIMA

The United States bombed Iwo Jima for two days. But the island was heavily protected and withstood the attacks. US forces wanted to capture the island to use it as a base for an attack on Japan toward the end of World War II. On February 19, 1945, US Marines landed on Iwo Jima. It was difficult for the men to move on the beaches, which were covered in volcanic salt. The troops and their machinery became stuck.

The Japanese did not strike right away. At first the US troops believed they had damaged the enemy defenses. But they were wrong. The Japanese were underground. They had established defenses in the island's natural caves.

The Japanese waited. Once more marines landed, the Japanese struck. Soon, the beaches were covered in damaged equipment and wounded and dead soldiers.

US Marines land on Iwo Jima, staying low to the ground to avoid being seen.

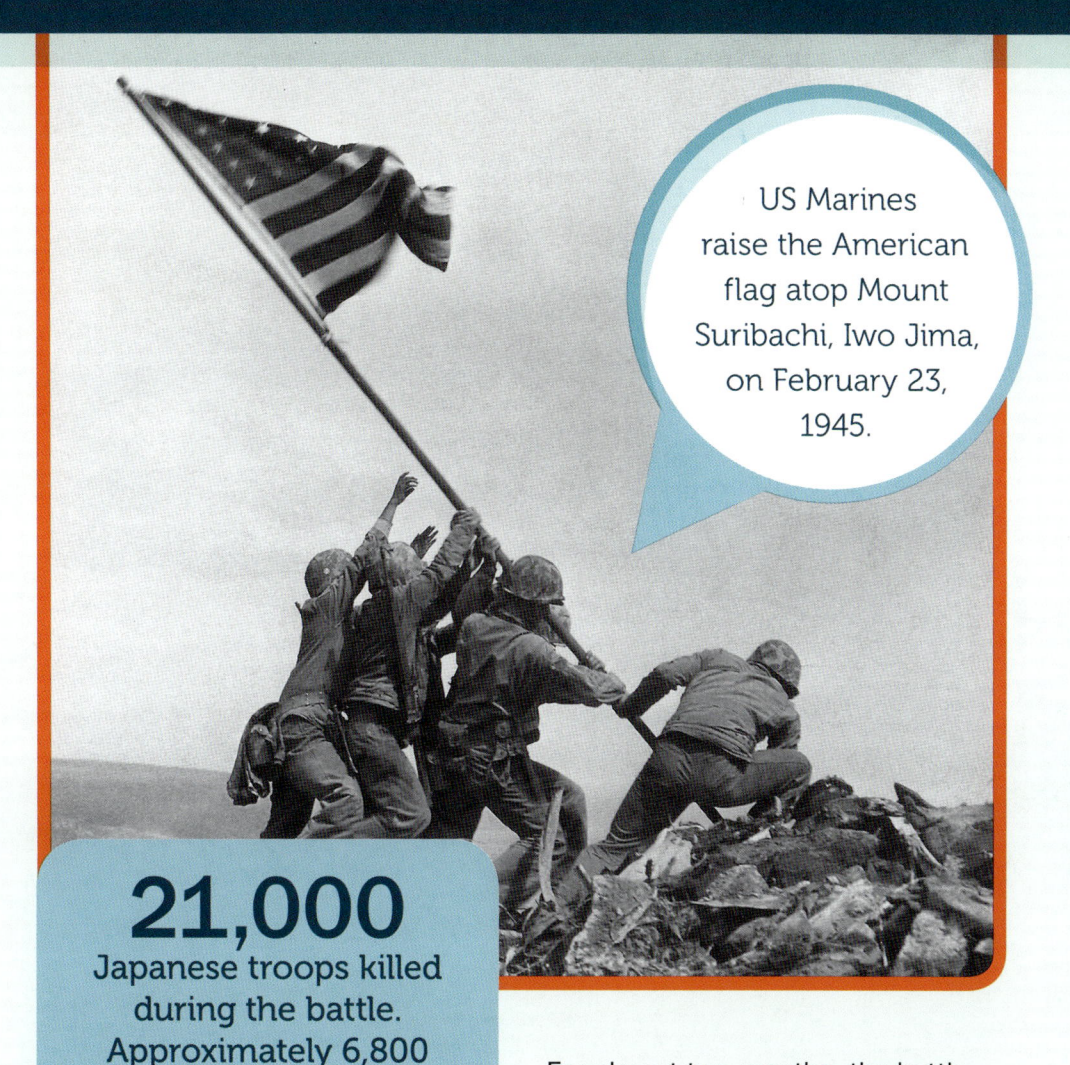

US Marines raise the American flag atop Mount Suribachi, Iwo Jima, on February 23, 1945.

21,000
Japanese troops killed during the battle. Approximately 6,800 US Marines were killed.

- February 16–April 7, 1945
- Approximately 75,000 US Marines invaded Iwo Jima.
- 22,000 Japanese troops occupied the military base.
- Approximately 1,000 Japanese troops survived and were taken prisoner.

For almost two months, the battle raged. Marines cleared out one bunker at a time. It was tough going. The Japanese troops used secret tunnels to sneak back into the bunkers. It took 36 days for the marines to take control of the island. After the battle, the United States continued its bombing of Japan, using Iwo Jima as a convenient base.

FACT SHEET

American Revolution

In the 1700s, Great Britain controlled 13 American colonies. Beginning in 1764, the British Parliament passed laws raising taxes in the colonies. This angered the colonists because they did not have representation in the British Parliament. The colonists declared their independence and fought the American Revolution to free themselves from British rule. The American Revolution ended on September 3, 1783, with the signing of the Treaty of Paris.

The Texas Revolution

In the early 1800s, Texas was a territory of Mexico. The Mexican government made land available in Texas to American settlers. By 1836, they outnumbered the Spanish-speaking Texans. Many Americans and Mexicans living in Texas became unhappy with Mexican laws. In 1835, they began fighting for independence. The Mexican Army led by General Antonio López de Santa Anna moved in to crush the rebellion. Texas declared its independence in 1836. It became the twenty-eighth state of the United States in 1845.

Plains Wars

The Plains Wars were a series of conflicts from the 1850s through the 1870s between Plains Indians and the US government. They were fighting for control of the Great Plains between the Mississippi River and the Rocky Mountains. The Black Hills of the Dakota Territory belonged to the Dakota and Cheyenne under the Laramie Treaty of 1868. Miners wanted control of the area after gold was discovered there in 1874. Congress passed a law forcing the Dakota and Cheyenne Indians to move onto reservations by 1876. After the Battle of Little Bighorn, US troops flooded the area. They killed many Plains Indians and forced the rest onto smaller reservations.

American Civil War

Abraham Lincoln was elected president in 1860. Soon after, Southern states began to secede from the Union over the issue of slavery. Eleven southern states formed the Confederate States of America. The 25 states in the North wanted the United States to stay one country. The Civil War between the Union and Confederate states lasted from 1861 to 1865.

World War II

World War II was fought from 1939 to 1945 in Europe and Asia. It began when Germany invaded Poland. Japan and Italy allied themselves with Germany. They were the Axis Powers. In 1941, the United States had not entered the war yet, but relations with Japan were worsening.

The United States stopped all trade with Japan. Japan decided to attack Pearl Harbor, which was home to the US Pacific Fleet. Afterward, the United States entered the war on the side of the Allied Powers. The Allied Powers included Great Britain, France, the Soviet Union, and China.

World War II fighting ended in Europe by April 1945. Germany and Italy surrendered to the Allied Powers. Japan would not surrender, although it was losing in the Pacific. On August 6 and 9, the United States dropped atomic bombs on the Japanese cities of Hiroshima and Nagasaki. On September 2, 1945, Japan formally surrendered.

GLOSSARY

bayonet
A long knife attached to the end of a rifle.

casualty
A person who is wounded or killed in battle.

colonist
A person who lived in one of Great Britain's 13 North American colonies.

colony
An area that is controlled by another country.

emancipation
The act of freeing someone from someone else's control.

militiamen
Citizens trained for military service.

mission
A group of buildings where people sent by the Spanish church lived and worked.

musket
A long gun popular during the 1700s and 1800s.

redcoats
A nickname for British soldiers who wore red uniforms.

reservation
Land put aside by a government for a group of people, such as the Native Americans.

scout
Member of an army whose job it is to collect information.

siege
When an armed force surrounds a building or army until it surrenders.

FOR MORE INFORMATION

Books

Asselin, Kristine Carlson. *The Real Story on the Weapons and Battles of Colonial America.* Mankato, MN: Capstone Press, 2013.

Beller, Susan Provost. *Battling in the Pacific: Soldiering in World War II.* Minneapolis, MN: Twenty-First Century Books, 2007.

Huey, Lois Miner. *Voices of the American Revolution: Stories from the Battlefields.* Mankato, MN: Capstone, 2010.

Josephson, Judith Pinkerton. *Who Was Sitting Bull?: And Other Questions about the Battle of Little Bighorn.* Minneapolis, MN: Lerner Publications, 2011.

O'Connor, Jim. *What Was the Battle of Gettysburg?* New York: Grosset and Dunlap, 2013.

Websites

American Battlefield Protection Program
www.nps.gov/hps/abpp/battleswars.htm

National WWII Museum
www.nationalww2museum.org

PBS: The Civil War
www.pbs.org/civilwar

The Library of Congress: Gettysburg Address
www.loc.gov/exhibits/gettysburg-address/ext/trans-nicolay-inscribed.html

INDEX

American Civil War, 14–15, 16–17
American Revolution, 4–5, 6–7, 8–9, 10–11

Battle of Antietam, 14–15
Battle of Bunker Hill, 6–7
Battle of Gettysburg, 16–17
Battle of Iwo Jima, 26–27
Battle of Little Bighorn, 18–19
Battle of Midway, 22–23
Battle of San Jacinto, 13
Battle of the Alamo, 12–13
Battles of Lexington and Concord, 4–5
Battles of Saratoga, 8–9
Burgoyne, John, 8–9

Cornwallis, Charles, 10–11
Custer, George, 18–19

Emancipation Proclamation, 14, 15

Gage, Thomas, 4, 6
Gates, Horatio, 8–9

Hooker, Joseph, 14

Invasion of Normandy, 24–25

Lee, Robert E., 15, 16–17
Lincoln, Abraham, 14, 15, 17

Pearl Harbor, 20–21
Pickett, George, 17

Revere, Paul, 5
Rochefort, Joe, 23
Roosevelt, Franklin, 21

Santa Anna, Antonio López de, 12–13
Siege of Yorktown, 10–11
Sitting Bull, 19

Washington, George, 10
World War II, 20–21, 22–23, 24–25, 26–27

About the Author
Anita Yasuda is the author of more than 80 books for children. She has written biographies, books about science and social studies, and chapter books. She lives in Huntington Beach, California.

READ MORE FROM 12-STORY LIBRARY
Every 12-Story Library book is available in many formats, including Amazon Kindle and Apple iBooks. For more information, visit your device's store or 12StoryLibrary.com.